BIGFOOT

FRIGHTENING ENCOUNTERS

BIGFOOT FRIGHTENING ENCOUNTERS

Compiled by Tom Lyons

BIGFOOT FRIGHTENING
ENCOUNTERS

Copyright © 2018 Tom Lyons

All information and opinions expressed in *Bigfoot Frightening Encounters* are based upon personal perspectives and experiences of those who were generous enough to submit them. Tom Lyons does not purport the information presented in this book is based on any accurate, current or valid scientific knowledge.

Acknowledgments

It's certainly no easy task for people to discuss their encounters with the sasquatch species. I'd like to personally thank the many good people out there who took the time and energy to put their experiences into writing.

BIGFOOT FRIGHTENING ENCOUNTERS

Out of respect for those who were involved, a few of the names have been altered or replaced with "anonymous".

BIGFOOT FRIGHTENING ENCOUNTERS

Would you like to see your report in an issue of *"Bigfoot Frightening Encounters"*?

If so, all you have to do is type up a summary of your experience, and email it to Tom Lyons at:

Living.Among.Bigfoot@gmail.com

Special Offer

If you submit a report and it is accepted, you will receive an exclusive paperback copy signed by Tom, shortly after the book is released. If you'd like to participate in that offer, be sure to include your mailing address in the cmail.

BIGFOOT FRIGHTENING ENCOUNTERS

Contents

BIGFOOT FRIGHTENING ENCOUNTERS

Introduction

Bigfoot Frightening Encounters"
actually came to be as a result of the
overwhelming feedback I had on my
original book series, *Living Among
Bigfoot.* It has been very interesting to
see how this book has developed very
organically over the past few months.

In fact, it all started shortly after the
release of the first book, when I received
a very kind email from a reader. After
congratulating me on the release, they
continued on to share with me their own
unique sasquatch encounter. Even after

having my own lengthy experiences with the fascinating species, I am still impressed by how truly healing it can be, to hear and read the genuine reports of others, especially when you receive them first hand. I suppose that irrespective of how visceral one's experiences with the species have been, a little part of you still needs further reaffirmation that these creatures are indeed among us.

Not long after I received the first reader recount, I received a second, followed by a third, and a forth. I can't emphasize enough how grateful I am to these folks for volunteering their reports for my own reading pleasure. However, eventually it seemed a shame for me to be the only one benefitting from all this additional insight. So, an idea occurred to me; why not compile a few of these texts into a publication so that other folks will be able to enjoy them just as I have?

The reports that you are about to read were all submitted by "Living Among Bigfoot" readers like yourselves and were selected to be featured in this publication. It is my hope is that this will be the first of multiple issues, as I think that hearing the recounts of others can have a very cathartic and therapeutic impact for those who have had encounters. Similarly, believers and sympathizers the world over can benefit from hearing the collective stories of those who know the truth; that these creatures are indeed among us.

-Tom

Report #1

My name is Glenn Barnett and I live on a small cattle ranch in north central Texas between the two small communities of Graham and Jacksboro, Texas. This is a very remote area with many hundreds of thousands of acres of largely uninhabited ranchland. We have several nearby lakes including one large one named Possum Kingdom. I grew up in this area and my memories of youth involved open fields, beautiful sunsets that lasted forever, and scattered groves of ancient oaks with smatterings of mesquite trees here and there. Over the years farming has stopped, ranchers have moved out, and the mesquite cutting and clearing has all but ceased. The mesquite trees have now become so dense that they actually form a large forest. I did not think anyone or anything ever changed here, but I have been proven wrong once again. The countryside is now lightly populated with rural homes, many seasonal creeks and lots of cover for wild animals...and people!!!

I have spent many years as a park ranger. I absolutely love the outdoors and all the inspiration nature provides. As a side note, I believe that it is from nature that we all get our greatest inspiration, and our greatest connection with God. I believe that when we live exclusively in cities, and surround ourselves with only man-made ideas and mechanisms, it allows our egos to grow out of control until we think we are the authors of all creation. By immersing ourselves in God's creations, we realize the smallness of ourselves and our ideas. It becomes much easier to gain perspective on ourselves and the world in which we live. When immersed in nature, the cyclical and interdependent nature of all that exists becomes far more observable than it ever could from inside a Volvo during rush hour in downtown Dallas.

But, I digress. I moved back to this area and to my family's ranch in order to take care of my elderly mother who refused to give up and move to town. I had several changes in my life, and it just seemed to be the right time to move to the country! I bought a nice mobile home and had it put down a few hundred yards from my Mother's house, so as to preserve each other's space and privacy. Many thousands of dollars later, I wished I had simply bought a travel trailer and put in in the back yard! All that aside, I enjoyed the house and it worked well being near Mother. The only drawback was employment; as I mentioned, we live in the middle of nowhere and because of this work is hard to find.

I have previously lived in small cities and rural communities, and for recreation I would find the most remote areas and go hiking and exploring at every chance I got. I have traveled and hiked over much of the United States, Canada, and Alaska. I even majored in Recreation and Parks in college. After hiking and wilderness camping in

Alaska I thought I knew wilderness. That is until I actually moved out into the country...

I spent the first six months being almost entirely outside, just listening to all the sounds. It was unbelievable to hear the sounds of nature without the low roar of traffic in the background (or foreground for that matter). Ever thought about the sounds that deer make? I always thought that they were largely silent as they are when being observed. On the contrary, their huffs, nighttime bawls, and sparring are fuel for the imagination. I learned the unique sounds of all the birds, frogs, insects and mammals both large and small. I can even tell the type of bird just by the sound of its wings flapping overhead.

The nightly and sometimes daily call of the coyotes change markedly with their moods and needs. I remember reading a story as a youth about an Eskimo tribe who knew that three white men were coming only by the calls of the wolves. I thought this preposterous. I now listen to the coyotes telling me if there is someone or something on the ranch, and where exactly they are located. If the coyotes don't warn me, the birds do. The deer will also let you know when something is out of place. I find it sad that due to the encroachment of civilization many of us can't experience the natural world anymore.

I never thought Sasquatch lived anywhere but the Pacific Northwest and wasn't even certain about that fact. I remember seeing the 'Patterson-Gimlin' film as a child, but did not give it too much though as it didn't seem relevant to my life in Texas. I became interested in the phenomenon later in life and have been fervently pursuing it for about 15 years. I remember flipping through the channels one night and seeing an episode of "Finding Bigfoot". I thought to myself, "finally, something worth watching."

I have read well over 50 books now, watched hundreds of hours of films and documentaries, and have become the local amateur sasquatch expert...for whatever that is worth! I frequently wear sasquatch T-shirts and it is amazing the stories people will come up and willingly volunteer. I would like to share a few of these with you, as well as my own experiences. I will keep it narrowed down to the area where I live, as it is definitely not well documented...

There is a very remote area in Jack County called Squaw Mountain. It is home to several big game ranches and a lot of native wildlife. After many casual conversations with a friend of mine at work about Sasquatch, we decided to take his wife and kids out 'squatching' one evening. We decided to head for Squaw Mountain, which we were drawn to both because of our lack of familiarity with the area and its remoteness. We call it "dirt roading" around here; we all climb in the truck and drive around on remote roads late at night in the hopes of seeing wild animals and such. It is really just a fun time to drive around and listen to the night sounds, identify a few constellations, get eaten by mosquitos, and tease the kids. On this particular night, we took a night vision camera and a listening device, as we thought we needed to appear serious about 'squatching' in front of the kids! It never occurred to any of us what would actually transpire.

There were four of us in the pickup that night. It is a crew cab by the way. We had been driving around for a couple of hours and had seen nothing but the usual hogs, coyotes, deer, rabbits, skunks, squirrels, raccoons, etc. You get the picture. We decided to stop alongside the dirt road and just sit for a while and listen, and so we found a place to pull off the road. The turnout overlooks a large field, a couple of small bluffs, and below that a heavily forested area runs alongside a small creek.

We were laughing, talking and passing around the aforementioned devices. So, eventually the night vision device was passed over to me. I had just recently acquired this device and was largely unfamiliar with it except for the basics of operation. I scanned out over the field and the creek bed and noticed nothing. I was about to hand it over, but decided to look around one more time.

I scanned across the creek bottom and into the field and noticed a black blob fairly near the tree line. It was quite large and not moving, so I assumed it was a cow or something that I had missed earlier. I focused the camera a bit better and realized it was an animal, but due to the large, rounded, shape of it, I suspected it was a yearling calf or a small cow laying down. I began to change the light settings on my device and turned on the infrared illuminator. The second I did this, the creature stood up! It became readily apparent that this was no cow. While facing me, it stood up straight, turned to the left, and took three steps into the tree line. I was absolutely in shock and couldn't believe what I had just seen.

This thing was enormous and moved more swiftly and smoothly than a big cat. It just flowed from one position to another. I was a tennis coach earlier in life and have been around many athletes. It takes incredible strength to move smoothly, and this thing moved unlike anything I have ever witnessed, tame or wild. I tried to hit the record button on my device but instead I accidentally turned it off. When I managed to turn the device back on- after a lot of cursing and much wrestling with seatbelts, door handles, etc. - the creature had vanished.

I tried to explain exactly what I had just witnessed, but of course, since I had the only night vision scope, no one else in the car had seen it. After we all settled down a bit, we all slowly inched out of our truck wearily to investigate the area. It was not our land, and trespassing can be very dangerous around here, so we were not able to search for tracks. We heard several strange owl type sounds but decided to call it a night. I wrestled for several days with what I had seen and decided to a report it to the BFRO. So, they came out and did a re-creation of the encounter.

I would like to share a few other much shorter experiences and reports from friends and acquaintances in the area. I had two other significant experiences on my ranch that I would like to begin with.

Last July -there is a pattern in this county- I had some friends over to watch movies late one night. We were all laughing and having a good time, when one of their kids jumped up from the couch. He screamed that he had seen someone, or something walk by my back window. My back window faces the ranch and is completely uninhabited for miles. Since I live so far out of town, this did not seem like it was even a possibility, so I just figured it was in his imagination. It is also pretty scary out here after dark!

Just to satisfy him and maybe all of us as well, we went out in the pasture to investigate. It was perfectly still, hot, and pitch black for miles in all directions. We shined the flashlight all around and of course saw nothing. However, we did encounter a strange smell that none of us were familiar with. It smelled kind of like a dead skunk, but not exactly. We quickly gave up on the search due to a lack of interest, skepticism...and the mosquitoes. The next day I let my dogs out to run around and I walked back behind the house. I walked up on three distinct human-like tracks, which measured about 16 inches long and 8 inches wide. The animal had literally walked within 25 feet of my house. Its trackway was visible and led directly to the creek right behind my house. To say the least I was surprised, since I had no idea anything like that was living in my yard!

A good friend of mine also saw what he described as an eight-foot-tall hairy looking man while 'coon hunting on my place in the mid 1990's. He said he never told anyone else about the incident, but he claims that he came within about 50 yards of the creature. He said he had heard a huge tree fall and pointed his flashlight toward the noise. When his light hit the creature, he said it was squatted down by the creek, but immediately stood up and took a couple of steps into the thick brush. He said it sounded like a freight train going through the dense underbrush.

He shared two other stories with me. He said in the early 90's he built a custom hog trap that measured about 7 feet tall by 6 feet wide. He said he had it placed on the aforementioned creek bed. After the initial setting, he returned to find it torn into four different pieces, with the huge metal door thrown over 100 feet away from the trap. He said the trap was several hundred pounds and was made from extremely thick steel wire and angle iron. He said what was done to it could not have been done by five or more men working together with equipment...

The second story involved the actual baiting and building of another trap similar to the one I just mentioned. He said he and his friend were finishing building a trap and baiting it after dark and were both inside the trap when something came up behind them. Apparently, it hit the door so hard that it slammed shut and knocked the trap completely over with them still inside of it. They never saw the creature but said it sounded like a train as it fled the scene. It took them over an hour to get out due to the damage that the trap had sustained.

Several people around town tell stories of strange wood knocks, tepee-like structures, and large rocks being thrown at them near Bryson Lake. All of this has occurred within two miles of my house.

Tom, I never would have imagined that these things could be this close to home, but in my quieter moments out here I realize it is entirely feasible that something could be hiding just behind the brush! Thank you for all that you are doing.

-Submitted by Glenn Barnett

Report #2

It was November of 1982 and I was 15 years old. I come from a hunting and fishing family and started to enjoy the great outdoors from a very young age. I harvested my first deer at 10 years of age. My father was a decorated WW2 Navy Veteran. He was actually on the US Yorktown and in charge of the engine room at the battle of Midway. He retired as a Master Chief, just to give you a little background about why I was raised to fear almost nothing. I think this also helps me to explain why I could never share this encounter with anyone, including my six older siblings; I was the youngest of seven.

It was a brisk November day. My father and I were out deer hunting in what was then the US Army Jefferson Proving Grounds. It is now known as Big Oaks Wildlife Preserve. My father and I had agreed upon ground stands and large trees that we would lean back against, which were big enough that if a stray shotgun slug happened to come your direction, the tree would stop it.

I had sat at my tree since 5:00 AM. At around 11:00 AM I ate the lunch that my mom had packed for me. It was a sunny day and it had warmed up to probably the lower 50s. Like any teenager with a full stomach, I fell asleep. I am not sure how much time had passed, but I was awoken by rustling footsteps in the dry oak leaves behind me. Thinking it was my dad coming to check on me, I leaned around the tree and froze.

Not 30 feet from me stood an ape-like creature on two legs. It had hair that I can only describe as being the color of ripe wheat. It stood approximately 9.5 to 10 feet tall. Its face was flat and was connected to what I guess you would describe as a high forehead. I did not get a great look at its eyes, but they seemed dark. I would guess its weight to have been somewhere between 400-450 lbs. I think it smelled the deer urine I had put down that morning, but with the weather warming up, the wind direction had changed.

Thank God, because I know in my heart that if it would have seen me... my family would've never seen me again.

I eased back around my tree and began to shake. I knew that the three 12-gauge slugs in my gun would do nothing to something that muscular, other than to simply piss it off. In a few minutes its footsteps gradually drifted out of earshot and I went to find my dad. I faked a stomach ache so that we could go home.

Years afterwards, I remembered that every year we would have to go to a safety briefing before the hunt and the Colonel would always tell us, "No cameras, and if you don't know what it is... don't shoot at it," before he would add, "You don't want to know what's in here." I have never told another living soul this story, and even after all these years. I'm still shaking as I think back on it.

-Anonymous

Report #3

The area in which these encounters took place is in in the Center Star community of Lauderdale County, Alabama. There are a mix of new subdivisions, farms, trailers, and old homes. It is very thickly wooded with plenty of deer, fox, turkey, livestock and other wildlife. The entire area runs along the Tennessee River with several large creeks branching off of the river. The Bluewater creek runs off the river inland and, in some parts, there are high cliffs and caves.

The main areas of focus for my recount are bordered by County Roads 33, 31, 411 and 111. There are plenty of areas where the woods get so thick that you cannot gain access to them. As a side note, there have also been some very large deer (14 point) killed here.

I will describe each incident in detail:

Incident #1

March 2011, about 7:00 A.M. It was the first morning of daylight savings, the clocks had been moved forward and I was out delivering papers. As I was making a delivery on road 33, I noticed a large herd of deer running across the road about 100 yards in front of me. I would see deer every night, so that wasn't out of the ordinary, but what caught my attention was that they were being chased. They crossed from the woods to the south into the thicker woods to the north. I pulled up and looked at the place where they had come out of the woods. I was searching for what had been chasing them, but the only thing I noticed was it was very still and quiet for that time of the morning, and the trees were shaking. I also noticed that some of the cows in a nearby field were acting funny... they seemed very nervous. I grew up around cattle so I can tell when they are out of sorts.

Incident #2

The next morning at around 5:00 A.M. I was on the backside of the woods where the previous incident took place. This time I was on road 411. This is a dirt road going down to the sailing club. It is very thickly wooded to the north and to the south are some weekend homes and the club. I only needed to deliver one paper, turn around, and drive back out. Although there is one street light at the end of the road, on the whole the street is still very dark.

I had stopped to use the bathroom. I was facing the woods as I was doing so and all of a sudden something growled and screamed out from the woods at me. It was close enough that it made the hair on the back of my neck stand up; it was probably within 20 yards of me.

I came back to investigate in daylight, and drove through the area slowly, but I didn't see or hear anything. I also did some research on bobcat calls, as that was the only thing I thought it could possibly be, but this was no bobcat call.

Several nights later I was in the same area, when suddenly about 200 yards in front of me I saw some eye shine coming from the river side of the road before crossing into the woods. The shine was about 6 feet high. I did see that the farm bordering this road had a large horse, and I knew that she had gotten out a few times, but she was nowhere near 6 feet off the ground. I began riding through the area with a video camera.

A few days later I saw the farm owner and I asked if she knew whether her horse had gotten out. She said she had not, but that her father-in-law said that was probably what had trampled all over the garden.

This whole area is very well-suited to a bigfoot. I called the woods "the bigfoot woods"; they just have a creepy feel to them. I began to check the area several times a day but never saw anything. A few weeks later, the landowner moved some cattle in but they did not stay long. I left a note on the fence asking if I could hike the area, but I never heard from him.

A few months later, we moved into a newer neighborhood about a mile away from our old property. This new neighborhood was on the river, so I was able to observe the area at several different times of the day and night.

Incident #3

Late August around 3:00 A.M. This encounter occurred roughly two miles from the first incident along road 111 closer to Bluewater creek. The area is an isolated road with thick woods to both sides. There are farms on either side as well. It was a very muggy night and I had my windows down and my tops out of the car. I was making a delivery and the area across the road from me sloped up slightly into some thick woods between two farms. The woods went all the way back to the creek and river inlet.

I had just made my delivery when I heard a sound that to this day is still the scariest thing I have ever heard. From across the road came this combination of a bark mixed with an owl hoot, followed by monkey chatter. It sounded like it was right inside the forest not far from the tree line, and judging by the array of noises I was hearing, I guessed that there were more than one of them. I left as quickly as I could. If something had come out of that slope it would have been right on top of me. I didn't see it but I felt its presence in the shadows just beyond the tree-line. I never took my tops out again on that road and kept my windows up unless I was delivering.

The next few nights I did slow down and listen as I drove through. I also began to patrol that area at several different times throughout the day. I noticed that the area had a small ditch running down the middle of it. I never found out who owned the land to explore it more. However, I did download some bigfoot calls and screams on my phone. While I was making deliveries, or at various times especially during dawn or dusk, I would ride through playing those calls. I never got a response.

There were several times I thought I heard hoots and calls. We had a lot of foxes in the area but I know they do not get loud. I heard these emanating from somewhere in the distance. Often while I was outside at night I would hear "screams" coming from the area of my first sighting. My new home was about a mile to the east of that area. I would also jog and run through that area but never saw anything else again.

I know that Lauderdale County has had a few sightings. I was directly across the river from Colbert County where they had some activity around 2000 (see GCBRO web site).

Wayne County, TN

This was around 1995-96 in an area of the county about ten miles inside Tennessee. This county has a lot of deep forest and timber, which enabled them to supply the paper mill in Courtland, AL with wood. I had been given permission to hunt a very deep area of woods by the land owner; he had said he never went all the way out there and that I could "have at it."

I began to prepare for deer season by doing some midday and late afternoon glassing. It was almost the perfect area to hunt; three miles off the main road, quiet and without any other activity for miles. The land next door was a huge cotton and soy bean field but looked like the "back 40" belonging to the land owner.

Incident #1

Early September around 5:00 A.M. on a Saturday. I decided to go to the location before sunset to set up. I found a spot overlooking the area I was planning to hunt, which enabled me to just sit, wait and watch to see what came through. I had a '78 Chevy Blazer so I was able to drive in about ½ mile from the location. I decided to walk the rest of the way in to cut down on noise.

I got there at about 4:00 A.M. and decided to sit and wait for a few minutes. I cracked my window a bit and noticed it was very eerily still... there was no noise at all. After a few minutes,

I got out to use the bathroom and noticed it was just way too quiet. I got the "willies" so to speak. A few minutes later something hit the hood of my Blazer...I thought it was just an acorn. A couple of minutes later a hand-sized rock hit the hood. I had my gun with me, so I loaded it and waited. Nothing else happened but I decided to leave anyway.

I came back that afternoon with my father but I did not tell him what had happened earlier that morning. We walked around and he noticed a tree was down. I remarked that I had been in the area last week and hadn't seen it. It looked as though it had been pushed over. We stayed about an hour and didn't see or hear anything. He was looking for deer signs, but I was looking for both signs of the deer and for something else...

Incident #2

About a week later, late afternoon at about 4:30. I was back in the area to do some late afternoon scouting and could see no sign of deer at all. I even sat in a very secluded area and did some rattling, but still there was nothing. I walked the perimeter, which ran along next to the neighboring land. The area I was in intersected with the cotton field and the start of a very thick growth of forest used by the paper mill. As I was approaching a very dense part of the forest, something huge broke out of the area but I could not see it as it moved so fast; it was gone in a flash. Whatever it was, it was huge. I have flushed deer before and this noise was so loud it sounded like ten deer. I kept waiting to see it break out of the woodline and burst into the field, but it stayed just within the perimeter of the trees. It was making a racket and I could see trees swaying. I also noticed a kind of musty, basement smell.

I hunted the land when the season started but never saw or heard any sign of a deer. I honestly think the area had been used so little that it had become nothing more than a "rest stop" for bigfoot. Maybe I had disturbed them. I went to the land owner and thanked him but told him that I had found another area closer to where I lived. He said, "Yeah, nobody has really had any luck back there...but I don't know why."

-Submitted by Bill Hogue

Report #4

Background Information:
Paul. Age: 50. Born in northern England. Resident of Catalonia, Spain for 30 years.
Jayne (my partner) age 49. Born in England. Resident of Catalonia.
Eric. Age 16. Born in Catalonia.
Sunny. (Jayne's daughter) Age: 13. Born in England. Resident of Catalonia.
Cookie. Age: 4. White Bichon Maltese.
Lola. Age: 5. Grey and white mini Schnauzer.

We live in the town of Torroella de Montgrí, 5 km from the Costa Brava coastline, where we also own and run a successful cafe bar. The population of our town is only 11,000, but doubles during the summer period.

For a short vacation I planned to hire a new motorhome and escape to the country as a way for us to disconnect from our very busy lives. We only had the option to go for three days and two nights due to the kids schooling. So, I made the plans for a weekend break this October. The new Ford motorhome was hired locally, and we set off early Friday morning. I reserved a spot at a rural campsite for the Friday and Saturday nights. These campsites only open on the weekends during this time of year. I didn't want to travel too far due to our very short time frame.

The Campsite "El Pont" is located near to the Pantano de Sau, which is a one hour and thirty minutes' drive from our home town. None of us had been to this place before. It is inland from the coast, away from the busy tourism of the Costa Brava, and actually feels like another country. The landscape is comprised of dense forests, mountains and of course the stunning lake/reservoir Pantano de Sau.

Friday was spent mostly setting up camp. The motorhome offered the luxury us townies require, but the rural campsite gave me the much-needed escape I desired after such a busy summer. Our rule was "no tech", so apart from Jayne, we all left our smartphones and tablets at home. This was to be very much a "back to basics" mini break. Jayne unfortunately had to take her technology as she also manages rental villas back home.

I have to say we all loved the place. The campsite grounds, although small in terms of the size of individual camping plots, actually spread across 10 hectares of dense forest, crystal clear streams, waterfalls, rock pools and even featured a stunning Roman bridge. Friday was a great day.

The next day (Saturday), the day of our encounter, started with a lazy breakfast and a pleasant dog walk. We set off mid-morning in the motorhome. The journey to the reservoir consisted of maneuvering the Ford beast around single-lane forest roads. During this 40-minute drive we saw numerous tin plate signs hanging from trees warning us about active hunters; this is the law here. I hadn't realized, but we were slap bang in the middle of the wild boar hunting season. Now these beasts are extremely common here and are called "porc sanglas" in the local Catalan dialect. These beasts can grow to huge sizes and can be extremely dangerous if they are in family groups. The large males and females are extremely strong, fast and will attack to defend their offspring.

Whilst driving, I mentioned to Eric that we'd be hearing gun shots throughout the day. Later, I also had a

quiet but very important chat with
Jayne.

The hunters had their 4-wheel
drives parked throughout the forest, and
I saw several men dressed in their
obligatory high visibility (Hi Vis)
clothing, with shotguns and several
hunting dogs.

We eventually arrived at the
reservoir and found a good enough spot
to park the motorhome for the day.
Our happy little family of four - plus the
two dogs - set off with our packed
lunches, tools and everything else we
thought we'd need for a day by the lake.
At this time, I warned Jayne that if by
chance we should come across any
startled wild boar we had to lift up our
dogs and stand dead still. This was to
signal that we pose no threat to them,

and in theory meant we'd be left alone, but I was still slightly concerned.

After a decent hike, we managed to escape the typical Saturday tourists, walkers and fishermen. I insisted we continued on a bit further and it was certainly worth the extra hike. We came across an idyllic location by the lakeside that would serve as the perfect base camp for the day. It was completely away from man or beast...or at least so I thought.

Now I must explain the overwhelming beauty of this place; it has sheer rock faces, dense forest, very red earth and crystal-clear water. In the middle of the lake there is an ancient village, and a church lies submerged beneath the water. During hot summers, when the water level is down, the village can be seen from the shores. It's a relatively popular tourist location, as the lake offers a chance to swim, cool off, and there are also kayaks for hire. In the off-season, the reservoir is very full and the area is quiet, which is exactly why I chose to come at this time of year.

Our wonderful Saturday was spent playing catch with our dogs, dipping our feet in the cool lake water, eating, drinking and generally lazing in the warm afternoon sun. Temperatures were good, and it was a stunning, idyllic day. The kids enjoyed whittling wood and making spears with the two pocket knives I'd brought along for just that purpose. I made a small fire by the lake edge, more for effect rather than heat, which certainly wasn't needed on such a stunning day. However, I did notice that I hadn't heard a single shotgun go off, nor had we heard any hunting dogs bark. In fact, we didn't see or hear another person or animal till around 4.00 p.m.

I was stretched out on the red earth enjoying the afternoon sun. The kids were with the dogs by the water's edge, and Jayne was answering a rental client's question via WhatsApp when she alerted me to the animal taking a drink from the water.

I turned to look and tried to focus on the thing by the water's edge. It was easily 100 to 150 meters further around the bank of the lake. As can be seen in one of my enclosed pictures, this is very rocky and backs up to the edge of the forest. I couldn't make out what I was seeing, but all I could tell was that it was hairy and reddish in color. My first thought was that it somewhat resembled a long-haired cow, native to the highlands of Scotland, but certainly not rural Catalonia. This thought instantly vanished when I watched a very human like arm scoop up fresh water, lake to mouth, time and time again. I could make out a huge mangy body of fur, a high forehead, huge shoulders and a huge arm and hand which continued to scoop up the water. I simply looked at Jayne and quietly mouthed, "what the f***?". The thing then glanced at me, making direct eye contact, before it rose up on two legs and headed back into the forest. Now, although it was big, it walked somewhat hunched over, and for some reason I thought it was extremely old; it walked like a pensioner and seemed tired.

We didn't alert the kids to this fact, but it instantly took the shine off the day. I wasn't scared in any way, but I couldn't quite figure out what I'd just seen. Was it some crazy mountain dude? A big guy in a suit? Whoever or whatever it was just didn't sit right. At this point, I said to the family that within the next 30 mins we should break camp and head back to the motorhome.

As little as 15 mins had passed when suddenly our two dogs went crazy. They are extremely good guard dogs, both very small but very brave pets. Suddenly they were both facing the forest, barking like crazy, but for the first time in my life they were backing up at the same time. All of us looked towards the forest and my first thought was that it could be a wild boar. We all tried to focus, when suddenly Eric shouted, "Dad, over there". He was pointing to a relatively open section of the forest. Then I saw it ... "big red". Now at this point I could clearly see the size of the thing. It's important to note that I'm 6ft 2 inches tall and my son is close to my height, but I know he'll be taller soon. We are both big guys, but from what I could gather this thing was easily over 7ft tall.

Both of us shouted in unison and we instantly headed towards the thing that was watching us from afar while the girls hung back and tried to calm the dogs. Whether this was fear or adrenaline kicking in, we both seemed to want to defend our pack and to confront whoever or whatever was stalking our camp from the forest. As we both scrambled up the rocks towards the forest, we could see it move back, retreating from our speedy approach. Jayne shouted after us, I can't say what she said to be honest, but I know I told her to "take f***ing pictures".

We were all heading through the trees, but now it seemed as if we were giving chase. I could see its red fur flash between the greenery as it took huge strides away from us. Jayne called out something else from the edge of the lake, the dogs were still barking like crazy, and were both starting to pant. We scrambled through another 100 meters or so of forest.

I came to a halt, and breathlessly I said to my son "I've lost track of it". As I tried to regain my breath, I caught sight of this giant face staring back at me with grey, aged features surrounded by mangy reddish fur. Its features appeared very much prehistoric; they were extremely ugly and big. It had also stopped, turned and appeared in front of me, maybe three meters away at most.

It stood there looking directly into my eyes, breathing heavily with its huge nostrils opening and closing, its fur-covered chest was rising in time with its massive inhalations. It was either also out of breath or it had decided it was time to fight. I now suddenly felt fear, I no longer wanted to be there or have my family put at risk. I was staring at something very old, very wild and a lot larger and heavier than me.

I calmly told Eric to start backing away slowly and he did exactly that while I maintained eye contact with the thing. I suddenly stumbled which made me move quickly as I tried to regain my composure, which added to my fear. At this point it seemed to almost grin at me, showing large but flat yellow teeth, very human-like in appearance only much bigger. I felt that it was smirking at me... that it could sense my fear.

I told Eric to turn and run when I thought that we were far enough away. So, we both ran until we made it back to base camp. I grabbed one of the spears the kids had made and told the family to move at speed. We quickly gathered our stuff, and with the dogs back on leads we made off. I constantly scanned the forest, fearing that it was coming after us. My heart was pounding, Eric was white in the face but said nothing at all. Sunny was a little tearful and confused, while Jayne bravely talked to us all as we scrambled back in the direction of civilization.

Back in the safe haven of our campsite, I did of course discuss this at great lengths with Jayne. We told Sunny it was just a mountain man and never mentioned it again in her presence. As far as Eric and I are concerned it has somewhat changed our lives. We saw and experienced a human-like beast that as far as we know has never ever been documented or mentioned. Is it a countryside secret? Do all or any of the locals know of its existence? Were the hunters actually looking for "it" rather than wild boar? The questions go on and on, and we discuss this on a daily basis. My son has started internet research which lead him to you, Tom. We are unsure of our plans or direction right now. Do we tell? Do we go back? Do we forget it?

I will say this though, just by writing this today I feel as though a huge weight has been lifted from my shoulders. It's the first day since the encounter that I feel almost normal again and may be able to concentrate on my normal life.

-Submitted by Paul and Eric Harvey

The photos are seen on the following pages.

The bright green tree is where Jayne first
saw the creature drinking from the lake.

One of the tracks next to a men's size 10 shoe. This photo was taken on a later day, about 40-50 minutes' drive from where the encounter took place.

The creature (near the center of the frame).

The creature (near the center of the frame).

Report #5

I haven't told many people about my encounter, but it's just one of those things I've never been able to debunk.

It took place shortly after school started in 2004, when I was 7 or 8 years old. My friend Travis, his older brother and I were riding our bikes at the dirt jumps, which still exist to this day. Suddenly, it started to storm. They left, but since my house was so close and for reasons that I still don't understand, I hung out by myself. I guess I just wasn't ready to go. Off to the right I saw this white figure moving slowly through the woods. It wasn't walking on a path, which I thought was strange. The first thing I noticed about the creature's physical appearance was that its arms stretched down to its waist and that it didn't seem to have much of a neck. It never saw me, but it walked through the brush, and past a tree stand that was in front of me. I'd say it was about fifty or sixty feet from me, and I can accurately gauge the exact distance because both the tree stand and the jump that I was sitting on top of are still there. Its shoulders came up to the platform of the tree stand, so I know it was taller than six feet, but it wasn't gigantic. Once it passed through, I rode my bike back to my house and told my gram about it, but of course she brushed it off and I didn't think about it much. That is until I was a few years older and saw a show about Bigfoot on T.V. Since then I've become pretty educated on the serious side of the bigfoot community, and I strongly believe that what I saw was a young bigfoot or maybe just a shorter one. As for the color of its fur, it seemed really odd to me until I started hearing about other sightings of white Bigfoot across Pennsylvania.

-Submitted by Matt Savino

Free Book

Are you enjoying the read?

Due to the unexpected success of this book series, I have decided to give back to the readers by making the following eBook **FREE** for anyone who wants it!

To claim your free eBook, head over to

www.LivingAmongBigfoot.com

and click the "FREE BOOK" tab!

Report #6

In 2013, my family decided to move to the mountains of West Virginia, about four miles from Plum Orchard Lake. We found our perfect little cabin nestled in the mountains on 10 acres, with a small creek that ran through the property. Behind our property were thousands of acres of state-owned land that were full of rugged beauty.

The first few weeks went by without any incidents, and we greatly enjoyed our new life. In that area of the United States, seasons changed faster than in our home state of Georgia. We noticed more and more wildlife getting closer to our house and around the creek. One of my friends came up to visit us and fell in love with the property. He enjoyed it so much that we ended up letting him put a tiny house at the bottom of the property in a clearing with a great view of the creek, about 50 yards from the main house. He ended up coming to work for me, and we rode there together every morning.

About a month after he moved to the property, we came home late one evening, pulled into the driveway and got out, only to hear the strangest noises coming from the ridge above the house. It sounded like something was pacing the ridge and making a loud blowing noise. We sat and listened for a few minutes. I thought it was strange but we parted ways and went about our separate evening routines. The next morning, I picked up my friend like usual, but he seemed shaken and extremely exhausted. I asked what was the matter and he said that tree limbs and stones kept hitting the side of his small house throughout the night. He seemed sincerely horrified.

A few days went by and my wife said she had this uneasy feeling while being outside, almost like she was being watched by something. She also said something was knocking things over in the yard. I began to suspect that maybe a bear was meddling around, since the area had such a high population of them.

That year we started getting our first snow fall around Halloween; something we were not prepared for being from the south. We spent a lot of the evening after that chopping logs on the very back of the property for fire wood. While back there we noticed what we thought were game trails down behind the house, which you could follow all the way to the creek. We thought nothing of it and continued collecting wood.

That night we started hearing something hitting our house. At first, it sounded like small stones, but then transitioned into what sounded like much larger rocks. I called my friend to see if he was messing around, but down the receiver I could hear the same noise of stones hitting the top of his house as well. We decided to see what was going on and to meet one another on my porch. I had my rifle and he had his. Both of our pits were with us. We grabbed our flashlights and headed toward the ridge. The dogs seemed extremely anxious. They were acting like something was close, but we couldn't see anything. All we found was a horrible odor and some disturbed stones around the house.

Thanksgiving came and went, and Christmas was fast-approaching. All the strange activity seemed to die down for a few weeks, that is until my friend got into my work van one morning and seemed completely freaked out. He said he had spent the entire night with his gun in his lap and his dog growling and watching his front door. He asked if I had heard anything the night before, and I explained that I'd slept like a baby. He went on to stress that something was messing with his front door and he said he was honestly scared to death. That weekend was like any other; we spent much of the time watching movies before heading to bed around 10:30.

Suddenly we were awoken at 2:00 in the morning by an alarming sound; "Boom, boom, boom!" It sounded like something was hitting the side of the house with a 2x4. My kids and wife were crying, and they all fled into our bedroom. I called my friend and he said that he could hear the sound from his place. I could hear his dog snarling in the background. We decided to get the guns and head outside to see what was going on. He ran up to my house and we set off into the woods. My dog was growling toward the tree line, so we headed in that direction. As we got closer, the dogs seemed afraid of something. We kept yelling out, "Who's there!?" The dogs then started barking loudly towards the trees next to us and we shined our lights in that direction. That's when we saw it.

I am over 6'2" and this had to be at least 8'8" or taller. Its hair was dark and matted, and when my light hit its eyes, they shined red. It was only there for a second, but time froze, and I absorbed every detail of the moment. It then stepped back into the thicket of woods behind it. The world became alive again and fear set in. My friend was screaming, "Did you see that!? Did you f***ing see that!?" What the f*** was that!?" I said, "I don't know man," and the urge to flee from the area quickly set in. We ran back down the property and something yelled out toward us; a roar unlike anything I had ever heard before. There was also the sound of pacing on the ridge. We both went into my house, locked the doors and sat with my family till morning. The next day my friend decided to move, and my family and I left in the spring...never to look back.

-B.B.

Report #7

In the early summer of 2014 I took a trip to the southeast Oklahoma mountain region with one of my sons and a friend. We had been told of sasquatch activity in that area and wanted to see it for ourselves. We settled in miles deep past the logging trails, and used that first day primarily to scout the area. We ran into a curious fox and a mother bear with two cubs that walked past our camp. We thought that if we made some noise it might make these creatures curious, which might bring them closer in. So, we set up some targets and fired off some rounds.

Later that night we heard what we could only describe as cat meows. Since we were in the middle of nothing but sticks it just seemed too odd. We also thought we heard what we guessed to be rocks hitting small branches, it was as if they had been thrown. That evening and the next morning all was quiet, either that, or we slept so hard that nothing could disturb us.

That day a thunderstorm passed through, and the sound of the echo was amazing as it bounced through the valley. We hiked around a bit but we didn't go too far due to the fact that we didn't know the area well. Light rains swept through all day. After a full day of searching we hadn't seen anything. We retreated back to our camp, and after supper I retired as the other two hung out by the fire. My friend brought his guitar and jokingly serenaded our hiding guest.

I was again soundly asleep, only to be suddenly awoken by my son. He was trying to not act too excited, but was frantically exclaiming "we have eye shine. Dad, wake up we have eye shine." I quickly threw on my boots without bothering to strap them, grabbed my sidearm and ran to where my compadres were positioned. We stood at the bottom of the steep sloping hill and a light rain began.

Approximately 30 yards up the slope, we could see occasional eye shine from behind a tree. We could also just make out what appeared to be a masculine shoulder and arm sticking out from around that same tree. My friend took aim and fired. In a flash, it looked as if the animal tried to grab the slug in midair, then it was gone. No sounds could be heard other than the firing of the gun and the light rain. Then to the left more eyes shone in the darkness, only this time they appeared orange, reflective and far larger; they were almost the size of tennis balls.

My son was standing next to me and suddenly yelled, "watch our six!" He had night vision with him, so he was able to keep watch of our sides and back. My friend said he was out of ammo and went back for more while my son continued his watch. What happened next still haunts me to this day. The creature charged us down the hill, but stopped 39 yards away, grabbed a large bush and shook it wildly. Then it stopped. The bush was 7 or 8 feet tall and then it stood up behind the bush. I was struck with fear. I could clearly see the shoulders, neck and head towering above the bushes. I had to remind myself to breathe.

Silently, I drew my 40 and fired three or four times. My son turned around with his night vision and caught a glimpse of the creature running up the mountain. It was moving quicker than he thought possible due to the light rain and the steepness of the slope. At this time, my friend had returned fully-loaded and we reported what had happened. My son also mentioned that he noticed what appeared to be blood on the foliage. We began to pursue what we assumed could possibly be a dead body, but we were quickly blocked by a cultural corral to our left, which stopped us in our tracks. We decided to stand there and wait, thinking it may not be a good idea to walk up on an injured creature. After several minutes of waiting we decided to climb the slope, but it was no easy task. We searched as we slowly ascended but found nothing.

We returned to camp for a long sleepless night. I was personally scared out of my wits that the creature would return. The next day, I decided we'd had enough, as I wanted to get my son out of harm's way. Even though he has had military experience, I still felt that I needed to do what I could to protect him. I've not shared this with very many people aside from close family and friends. Why would I fire on a creature, you ask? Well it's quite simple; no specimens... no creature. I believe these creatures are related to the Gigantopithecus that crossed the Bering Strait. I personally call them "Wood Apes". But, without a body we have no real way to prove their existence.

-Submitted by Papa John

Report #8

This terrifying and confusing experience happened on a typical summer night at my grandmother's house in Winston, Georgia. So, at around 11pm eastern time, me and some of my buddies were hanging around outside. To give you a better visual of where this sighting took place it's important to know that my grandmother's house is surrounded by trees on all sides except for in the driveway. On the left inside the driveway at the bottom of the hill there is a ditch that we put cut up branches and tree leaves in. During this frightening encounter, we were standing at the top of the hill between the house and the van. We were chilling outside next to the van for at least an hour and a half and during that whole time I never saw or heard anything go into the ditch. Then all of a sudden, a big somewhat human, bear-like creature crawled out the ditch and stood up two legs. It bolted down and out of the driveway and headed toward the left side of the road. Startled, I repeatedly yelled, "Hey who is that? What are you doing here?" The creature didn't even turn its head or anything.

If I had to describe the creature, I would say it was over 7 feet tall and very bulky. From where I stood, it looked as though it had thick, wooly, black hair or fur. Its neck and shoulders were not at a right angle like a person's, but rather it was almost rounded where the neck and shoulders touched.

I started to chase after it as I really wanted to solve the mystery, but then my gut forced me to stop because I had no clue what I was getting myself into. When it ran to the left, I imagined that it probably ran through the woods to the train tracks. I haven't seen it again since then. Ever since, I prefer not to walk alone in that neighborhood at night. I've even bought a trail camera and I will be sure to let you know if it ever comes back again...but I really hope it doesn't.

-Submitted by Isaac Shackleford

Report #9

It was July in Miami County, Ohio. There is a river that runs past our aquatic center which is a popular fishing spot for the locals. It was a warm day so we decided to take a trip to the fishing spot.

We were fishing on a trail off the path into the river and I was about 15 meters away from my friend who was fly fishing. I looked up after catching a whiff of this horrid stench, and saw a 7-8-foot-tall creature with brown shaggy fur stand up and growl. Then, I suddenly heard a tree fall behind us. We booked it as fast as possible to the truck.

The next day we returned to the area and saw snapped limbs and the fallen tree, but we could tell that it was still green and alive when it fell. We believe there were more than one of the creatures; two to three based on how the tree fell.

Also, I should mention that there were large paths that had been trampled into the ground that led from deer trails to other parts of the forest, which hadn't been there the day before.

-Submitted by Noah Barnes

Report #10

I grew up in the Southern Tier region of New York, specifically, in Allegany County. It is an area of farmland, forest and is sparsely populated. There exists a local legend of bigfoot with all the usual Hairy Woman nomenclature attached. The Klipnocky state forest backed on to our property and featured both CCC-planted trees and natural hardwood trees, making an area that totaled under 2,000 acres. There are natural limestone caves, creeks, dirt roads winding through the hills, and a large population of deer, game birds, plants, etc.

My first experience with the hairy woman occurred when I was five or six. While picking wild strawberries with my mother, I had run out in front of her when I heard something heavy jump out of a trcc. I froze. Heavy, slow footsteps could be heard heading in my direction from approximately two hundred yards into the red pine woods. Terrified, I ran back to her and together we both headed home.

In the years since then I have spent a lot of time hiking and camping in these woods. I would often hear the Hairy Woman treading lightly through the campsites where my friend and I camped many times. Usually more than one would come by at night. They would whistle quietly to each other as they traveled through. I'm not sure about knocks but it is possible that I heard them.

People in this area would talk about seeing and hearing them while hunting and driving through. Their existence was widely known and accepted, and there was never any negative talk about the Hairy Women being dangerous. I remember that everyone just took this animal to be part of the woods like all the other animals.

This story ends with a night when I was 21 or so while out cruising around with a friend. We were out near an old gravel pit, which is about a 1/4 mile from the house I grew up in. It was late, and we were just quietly talking and dozing off when I heard what sounded like some heavy animal walking down one of the sides of the pit. I could hear stones sliding down and a sound that was the scariest and creepiest noise I've ever heard; it almost sounded demonic. We sped off without looking back.

Years later, I wondered whether it could be the same bigfoot I had heard years earlier. In fact, we were only several hundred yards from where my first experience had taken place.

-Submitted by Dave Thompson

Report #11

I want to preface this by stating that I
am going to summarize a few of my
family's encounters with these creatures.
As of today, I have documented 61
different incidents. I did not start
keeping a journal of these personal
accounts until almost three years after
my first eyewitness encounter; if I had
started earlier, the documented
incidents would have far surpassed 61.

Initially after my first encounter I was so "shell-shocked" that I now realize that I had developed PTSD from the event. During a roughly three-year period after the first encounter, my wife and I had numerous unexplainable things happen to us at our home. However, I never thought to start documenting the events for future reference. It was only after speaking with a friend that I decided to take their advice and start keeping a journal.

My wife and I are both college graduates; I have obtained a master's Degree in Adult Education and she currently has a degree in Education with a minor in English Literature. In my prior job, I was often called upon as an expert witness to provide testimony in high profile criminal or civil cases. We are both very aware of spinning tall tales and what it could do for our reputations.

In the Fall of 2008, my wife and I moved to rural southern West Virginia and built a small log home in a sparsely populated area. We have approximately twenty people living within a five-mile radius of us. Our property sits adjacent to a 13,000-acre wildlife management area, and in addition to the 20 acres of land that we own, I also lease another 800+ acres for hunting.

In the summer of 2009 my wife fell extremely ill from a failed kidney. She was in and out of the hospital for several months during this time. After my wife had been released from the hospital to come back home, she was very weak and stayed in the bed most of the time. During this time our little girl was barely two years old and our son was seven years old. My wife and little girl had laid down for a nap, and my son was in his bedroom, most likely playing a video game. I was sitting on our front porch working on an electrical corn feeder head that had recently been torn up, when I heard a rather loud shriek coming from across the mountain on top of the ridge adjacent to our home. Both of my basset hounds heard the shriek and they began to growl deeply. Their fur bristled on end while they looked toward the mountainside.

After a few moments of silence, I distinctly heard what sounded like a huge object crashing through the brush coming off the hill from the ridge toward our house. The sound was loud, but it was also slow and methodical. It was almost as if something the size of an elephant was walking in the brush toward me. The dogs continued to growl, and grew more and more unsettled. I stopped what I was doing and started watching the woodline curiously. As the moments passed, the object responsible for the noise continued to get closer to our home, as it walked in a straight line off of the ridge. I realized that at any moment I would be able to see the culprit responsible for the racket, so long as it continued to walk in the direction it had been heading.

I observed our dogs. They had retreated from our yard and had attempted to hide themselves in a large hole in the hillside that ran alongside our front yard. The hole was there due to me up-rooting a tree earlier in the year. Finally, I could make out a large, hair-covered "thing", standing on its hind legs, as it stepped out of the wood-line and looked straight at me. The creature was approximately 60 yards away from my position and was standing in clear view of me without any obstructions. That past spring, the local power company had contracted a brush cutting company to clear out all the underbrush adjacent to the powerlines. The creature was standing in this clear-cut area.

When I first observed the creature, I immediately attempted to process what I was seeing. My first thought was that it was a bear, standing on its hind legs. I further convinced myself that it made sense for me to be seeing a bear because I had two full trash cans sitting at the base of the hill near the road. This thought was further confirmed when the creature squatted down toward the ground, because I convinced myself that the bear had sat down on its rump. After the creature squatted down, it became completely motionless. It was so motionless that it literally melted into its surroundings. Had I not been looking straight at the creature as it squatted, I most likely would have never seen it in plain view.

After the creature sat motionless and observed me for several moments, I became bored with looking at the "bear" and I went back to tinkering with the electronics I was working on. After a few minutes, I noticed movement in my peripheral vision. I looked toward the movement and I witnessed the creature stand back up. At that moment, I knew that I wasn't looking at an odd-shaped, overgrown, dark brownish-black bear; I was looking at what I thought at the time was a "monster." The "monster" turned side profile to me, while keeping its eyes locked on me the entire time. This is when I really got a good look at the creature, and I then knew without any doubt that I was looking at a "monster" and not a bear.

The creature was between seven and eight feet tall with a thick chest and large, long arms. The creature's waist was thick, and its legs and hips were extremely sturdy and powerful. I could not make out any facial features because of the distance, but I could see the brow ridge and eye sockets, as well as the oddly colored skin that didn't have hair.

The "monster" proceeded to walk from my left to right while maintaining eye contact with me the entire time. It proceeded to walk a parallel line to my right for approximately one hundred and fifty feet and it entered a pine thicket across the road from my front yard. The creature stopped as it entered the thicket. It proceeded to make the loudest and most guttural roaring howl I had ever heard, which could never be replicated by a human being. The roar reverberated throughout my chest and it literally felt as though it shook my porch.

I began to panic, and I imagined that the creature was going to attack our home. Suddenly, the creature let out the most ghastly, ungodly moaning howl that could only be dreamt up in someone's worst nightmares. As the creature's howl started to taper off, I could hear a low growl emanating from it. I could feel the reverberations from the growl, and I grew weak at the knees as it sent a chill down my spine. I left the front porch area of our home and proceeded to arm myself. I thought of calling 911 but I realized that they might think I was either intoxicated or just a basket case.

Needless to say, I could go on and on about events that happened after this initial incident but, let's just say that I became afraid of going outdoors for quite some time. I am an avid hunter, and I have been published in a popular hunting magazine for some of my trophy kills, but I became terrified of the woods after this. For the longest time following this incident, I had managed to block much of it out and forget about it.

Gradually, after talking to friends and doing a lot of research, I was able to start regaining some "normalcy" in my life again. Only after I re-entered the woods, and started hunting and fishing again did I fully remember the events that happened during this life-altering encounter.

Obviously, I have had many, many more things happen since then, but this was the first time that I consciously realized what was happening to our family. Finally, I had an explanation for so many strange events that had been happening to us and our home since moving into the area where we still reside. Additionally, I became an instant internet junkie as I tried to find any and all information that I could on the subject of sasquatch. The more I discovered, the more I realized I was experiencing the same things that many people elsewhere had reported happening to them too.

After my incident I learned through some "unofficial" investigative work that there have been a multitude of sightings and encounters in the area for years. Some of the local names for the beast are "The Redeye" or the "Booger." Another popular name used by old timers was "The Devil." Supposedly, they even found the nest of one of the "Devils" back in the 60's. The place is still referred to as "The Devil's Den." It is a large cave that is in the heart of the wildlife refuge. The Devil's Dens is within two miles of my current residence.

Coincidentally, there is a documented account of a local school bus driver who claims that a creature ran off the hill on two legs and jumped from the hillside onto the roof of her bus. It happened while she was parked adjacent to the hillside while she was waiting to pick kids up for school. The driver claims that she heard something running off the hill and she exited the bus to see what the commotion was all about. According to the report, the woman claimed a "werewolf" looking creature that was covered in hair, and seven feet or taller, ran on two legs down the hill and jumped onto her bus as she quickly re-entered it. The driver said she sped away with the monster still on the roof of the bus, but that she was uncertain as to where the creature finally came off the top of the bus. Needless to say, the lady went straight back to the bus garage and promptly reported the incident and then quit her job. The location where the lady had parked happened to be down the hill on an old dirt road just below the Devil's Den.

-Submitted by George and Chasity Kennedy

Interested in Tom's experience with the sasquatch species?

The popular "Living Among Bigfoot" series is now available!

Editor's Note

Before you go, I'd very much like to say "thank you" for purchasing this book.

I'm aware you had an endless variety of bigfoot-related books to choose from, but you took a chance on my content. Therefore, thanks for reading this one and sticking with it all the way to the last page.

At this point, I'd like to ask you for a *tiny* favor; it would mean the world to me if you could leave a review where you purchased this book.

Your feedback will aid me as I continue to create products that you, as well as others, can enjoy.

Mailing List Sign Up Form

Don't forget to sign up for the newsletter email list. I promise this will not be used to spam you, but only to ensure that you will always receive the first word on any new releases, discounts, or giveaways! All you need to do is simply type the following URL into your internet search bar.

URL-

http://eepurl.com/dhnspT

Social Media

Feel free to follow/reach out to me with any questions or concerns on either Instagram or Twitter! I will do my best to follow back and respond to all comments.

Instagram:

@living_among_bigfoot

Twitter:

@AmongBigfoot

About the Editor

A simple man at heart, Tom Lyons lived an ordinary existence for his first 52 years. Native to the great state of Wisconsin, he went through the motions of everyday life, residing near his family and developing a successful online business. The world that he once knew would completely change shortly after moving out west, where he was confronted by the allegedly mythical species known as Bigfoot.

You can email him directly at:

Living.Among.Bigfoot@gmail.com

Made in the USA
Monee, IL
02 April 2023